Safety Sand

Also by Garry Thomas Morse

POETRY
  After Jack*
  Discovery Passages*
  Prairie Harbour*
  Streams
  Transversals for Orpheus

FICTION
  Death in Vancouver*
  The Chaos! Quincunx series
    Minor Episodes / Major Ruckus*
    Rogue Cells / Carbon Harbour*
    Minor Expectations*

* Published by Talonbooks

SAFETY SAND

GARRY

THOMAS

MORSE

TALONBOOKS

Talonbooks
278 East First Avenue, Vancouver, British Columbia, Canada v5T 1A6
www.talonbooks.com

First printing: 2017

Typeset in Albertan
Printed and bound in Canada on 100% post-consumer recycled paper

Interior and cover design by Typesmith
On the cover: Amadeo de Souza-Cardoso, *A chalupa* [*The Sloop*]
(*circa* 1914–1915), oil on canvas
Page 1. Untitled photograph by Stasja Voluti

Talonbooks acknowledges the financial support of the Canada Council
for the Arts, the Government of Canada through the Canada Book Fund,
and the Province of British Columbia through the British Columbia Arts
Council and the Book Publishing Tax Credit.

LIBRARY AND ARCHIVES CANADA CATALOGUING IN PUBLICATION

Morse, Garry Thomas, author
  Safety sand : poems / Garry Thomas Morse.

ISBN 978-1-77201-198-2 (SOFTCOVER)

  I. Title.

PS8626.O774S24 2018   C811'.6   C2017-907319-2

On the prairie there is a chairman's chair
I will sit in the chair
and the public will be at my feet
It will be warm it will be cold

—BENJAMIN PÉRET

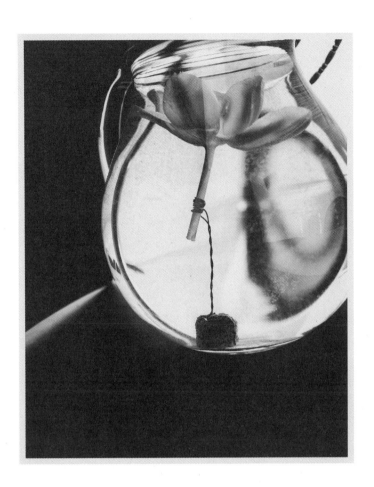

LET IT SLIDE[*]

---

[*] Transmutation of "Laissez passer" by Aimé Césaire.

Facile prolongation of swallow reflex by the obscene hermetic
    mouth
this dark prolific muck
reflux of gluey herbal carnivores hearing within sticky pedicels
    bonding news
deemed necessary in this world choked by a grim *idiotwind*
masking the verve of yellow inversions

Crutch crutch over vertiginous abyss
crutch crutch over nothingness
crutch crutch over inferno

but even mid-air I meet a thousand whetted knives
a thousand cruel lassos a thousand sacerdotal crows

roar strike rock and sand I people with fish
let logos loom over factories
echo your collaborator echo your fiery redux
echo your silvery soapbox
echo your rails and derailments
echo your electrified utensils
echo your moronic togs
echo your spidery horizon
echo your gleaming porcelain
echo your tidy chattel ripped apart by catastrophe
echo your groans
echo your drones
I endure along unmarked parallels the procession of dim-witted
    tourists
whose mammalian trail perpetuates untold forest ticks
backwater
agitation
finical cougars give their lip-curling grimace at the very scent of
    me the air
halts I hear the grinding of each pole on its ambiguous axis the
    air snarls

projectile dysfunction stalls the decolonization of my mind the
    air bears
living river like a lover deep into my lungs fit to bursting
cedar chopped up into ridges the skeletons of ancient
flounder stuck in the sediment like a totem
caught in similarly murky times
carved by a tribe
of next to

FUNEREAL
COCOONS

Carcass[*]

Light of my life, remember
that warm February morning
that charming carcass
on the cracked ice

Bare legs had petrified in the air
and we made hushed assumptions
once that noxious stench
sank in our cynicism

Blinding sun shone down on
that putrid flesh, where the glow
of a scarlet globemallow motif
was beaded on mukluks made

overseas or possibly nearby
a thought like the thaw that
roused our equinoctial optimism
along with larval colonies

that rose and fell
in an ominous wave
in the last breath
of that ruined body

Indeed, it was life-affirming
to heed such pestilent music
to see the manifest destiny
of a vanquished race

Then its shape altered
to satisfy our appetite
for exquisite corpses
in MISSING sketches

---

[*] Transmutation of "La charogne" by Charles Baudelaire.

Never had the urban beasts
hungered for such fodder
not since a few centuries ago
for the vanishing savage

What can we do but revel
in that wretched woman's fate
her arrow aimed no higher
than an open grave

Living is now such a luxury
one can do no more than prepare
for this abominable honour
and they will sing your name

as beaks tear into your skin
red petals on a dying prairie
where a Mourning Cloak
punctuates melting snow

Unluck[*]

Schlepping such futile weight
(even *The Myth of Sisyphus*)
can only help you so much
as Art is long and Time is short

according to that hackneyed
cliché although I cannot say —
my heart is a heavy drum
confiscated long ago

another fractured arte-
fact in dusty shadows
of a vacuous museum

toxic as milkweed host
hiding translucent eggs
full of bright survivalists

---

* Transmutation of "Le guignon" by Charles Baudelaire.

Flask[*]

Certain agents disintegrate
all matter ... penetrate
whatever they overlap
with the mysterious

potency of a tomb
withholding fatal
secrets, sealed with
psychical fortitude

where a thousand thoughts
sleep, funereal cocoons
that take to the air
outrageously

reborn as oily symbols
for transient mortality
in stolen masterworks
from another age

instead of sorely
troubled corpuscles
and grim afflictions
of urban miasma

As for my own
brand of nastiness
may you one day
distill an antidote

from stray DNA
within this sepulchre
and let it soothe
wherever it scars

---

[*] Transmutation of "Le flacon" by Charles Baudelaire.

Wounded Bell[*]

How bittersweet to warm oneself
on a winter's night, reflecting on
furtive manoeuvres that brought
the wounded bell back to us

Agents and unmarked copters
circled in the heads of heroes
while behind dark glasses
their eyes dilated wildly

out of fear you would fail
to fondle that fogey bell
with a lover's tenderness

or worse, smother its glory
with your heart still haunted
by the oblivion of battle

---

* Transmutation of "La cloche fêlée" by Charles Baudelaire.

Evening is our accomplice
stealing in like a coywolf
right before the sky closes
and we turn into beasts

Evening, affable evening
sought by the sorest eyes
with all desire dried out

Evening soothes silent grief
and calms the unconventional
as shattered bodies collapse
as sleek demons arise
intent on nocturnal business
then twist the blinds shut

Loyal to the patriarchy
our sex trade revives
its flagging dialogue
about missing sisters
for a common enemy
brutes in uniform
who would sooner beat
or abandon someone
to die than quit trolling
for more torture porn
as smashed windows
startle out of sleep
antique fantasies of
chattel and pillage
our grim subsistence

---

* Transmutation of "Le crépuscule du soir" by Charles Baudelaire.

Did I ever have a soul
to "Indian-give" away
at this desperate hour
when sickos are sapped
by enervating fetishes
and fatidic visions
amid hollow death
rattles of the destitute

more mortifying statistics
for lives without a home

Heaps of Nothing[*]

Mournful mind, once deluded
enough to believe that manic
ride would go on forever
and never crash awkwardly

Sleep, cortices, sleep reptilian sleep ...

Vanquished mind, old marauder
love has become little more
than the frail kind of spark
that starts insurance fires

Suck up that stink of artifice ...

Time swallows me slowly
the way this thick snowfall
digests poor snowflakes
that prey upon the brain

Then nothing, only nothing ...

---

[*] Transmutation of "Le goût du néant" by Charles Baudelaire.

Skeleton Labourers[*]

1

On nanoscopic surfaces
in unrecycled slag heaps
encoded cries for help
slumber without hope

once warmly backlit
with countless images
that inundated the
eyes with optimism

not these horrors
glued to the glares
of gaunt labourers
longing for the end

---

[*] Transmutation of "Le squelette laboureur" by Charles Baudelaire.

2

Resigned automata
what weird harvest
will be reaped
from sly hacks

or those pretty
sleek devices
released from
damaged flesh

with medical
mask emoji
to deny any
last benefits

since Death
only doubles
company lies
in disclaimer

leaves you
in waste lands
salvaging gold
mercury, enamel

To a Passerby[*]

A nauseating street was hurling
noise when a woman passed by
in the manner of a racy banner
censor to her own provocation

in each shiver of a statuesque
meme that made one eye roll
redden, rove, twitch, and
bulge with sweet torment

then she accidentally flashed
warped proportions with the
calibre of online distortions

prompting diurnal emissions
that were soon swallowed up
by that street of muffled love

---

* Transmutation of "À une passante" by Charles Baudelaire.

Toward an Epilogue[*]

With the sagacity and sanity
of reflection on tranquillizers, I
launch into heated declarations:

Often ...

your debauchery and dirtbaggery
your flirtations and love affairs
that lacked satisfaction
your illimitable desire
that popped up
                everywhere

your bombs, your blades
your hoots, your holidays
your depressing suburbs
your no-tell hotels
your parks packed with intrigues
your sickly places of worship
your prolonged childhood
your discouragements

your fireworks and eruptions
that populate your empty sky
your materialistic vices
your moral exhibitionism

your rigid principles and bent rules
your haughty monuments in the haze
your dull greenish domes
your divas stripping down
your musical explosions
your fake barricades

---

[*] Transmutation of "Épilogue (II)" by Charles Baudelaire.

your inane orators and their rhetoric
that flows with the blood of others
beyond our frigid roads and rivers

your bedraggled buffoons who speak truth

Beings the colours of butterflies
slurping up the disturbing sweat
and elbow grease of my alchemy

extracting the quintessence of everything

Yes, I have made the most of your muck

ORPHÉE
THROUGH
GLASS

Erasure

Sleep your way through history and see if we care. No need to get allegorical just yet. The night is young and legal. Listen, the night is full of night life.

When the professor ambled through vanity in cleaning gloves s/he was neutered in terms of possibility. The piece of paper arrived via a system of relays on automatic. The letters of the piece of paper promised that nothing would happen (again).

When we saw Cégeste with his vintage vacuum, we knew he was not going to make it. He was young but legal.

A fantasia in Beethovenish raptus
concealed that natural beet sugar

rang in our ears true and clever
borborygmus of hyperbolic blurbs

While an inflammatory dissertation
on concert music went on, we wept
for Glück, cramming love into cleft
the way we cram love into couplets

According to Criterion, the couplets refer to Cocteau having crammed his poetic cock into Orphée in the pluperfect and cramming his poetic cock into Cégeste in the present tense. Such tension is still palpable on the surface of the celluloid acetate and Cégeste snorting at Orphée is his endowment to classic film (and myth).

Jane Rule sagely points out that Violette Leduc wore one to be noticed.

Turning it off excruciates
Turning it on agitates
Condemnation. This life of
being eternally reachable
Leave a message at the—
In you I crash cars
Is that you or me
Leave a message at the—

Cégeste is hella chuffed over his ciphers. Take the piss out of him and I mean yesterday. We would polish him off if that did not precipitate an air of even more redundancy.

Orphée accepts his pink slip and swaggers off. The Princess forgives him (quelle surprise). She will suss out what can be arranged at Dollarama.

A telegram sings that Samuel Beckett just lay down for the Resistance. Stop. This system of contradictions is capable of producing such a cock-up we win the war. This Gestapo chic is ours for the taking.

Poke
the vicious scrape of a rake
that does its business
beneath these bare trees
ceding seas
crows and garbage trucks
not giving a Gluck
his due till the Forks is turned into constellation
still aching for
present participles

The Poet stirs in bed on account of garbage trucks that haul away excessive reams. This is the most important occurrence in the history of Osborne Village. Bacchantes battle waste collectors for the spoils but lose to wasps.

Meanwhile, back in the archive, James Reaney regales the others with tales of a cat who plays his operas in Central Park. Canada's long poem nearly awakens from its coma.

Orphée was just brought downtown for eight counts of Indian Rope Burn and one noogie. Interrogation did not nail him for possession of "Canada."

Soon she knew
dreams were the least interesting
aspect of sleep. Soon she
pinched the pair of long underwear and
turned a profit
just as Orphée awoke, panicky
thinking he had eaten
                   'em

again

When the Comtesse bid generously, the Princess knew that Orphée had perused pleather upon pleather of *that woman* at his leisure.

The day she decided to Swipebuster his Tinder logjam was a dark one. She was obliged to delete his permissions.

Orphée is still on a miracle crash diet and still cranky.

A permit for our lobster on a leash
looks askance at steaming sequitur
The day goes faster that way
boiled in a steamy pot

Territory sales need propping up
in the region we dare not name
where future captains of industry
take down scrummy particulars

This is a celebrity recipe for a land claim. The Poet would like to
express what the good doctor saw in the Utrecht Psalter, or his
stash of comely pornographemes that never knew light of day nor
the kiss of an innocent.

Orphée is still washing dishes and singing. Eurydice spends her
evening on a public gallery of everything they ate.

The dupe
does not mean to replace
that resplendent goop
that surrounds
The dupe is a dummy company with a mission statement
about tremendous inertia and a seasonal catalogue about
every kind of goop under the sun
It is not unusual
for the dupe to harass us
during a flex break

The dupe is a diabolical company that caused our margin/ally
popular meltdown. Between you and me, the goop is still awaiting
FDA approval.

Not to be confused with a very special episode about The Gooch,
which validated Rainer Maria Rilke's valiant struggle with the
visible and the invisible.

The dupe maintains the finest glorywall in this hemisphere.

On some level the
Greyhound to Brandon, Manitoba
could be a game-changer
Did something happen
while you were away, ask the
Wheat Kings, with the kind of concern
they usually reserve for
snipers

You know, when the Poem is this alone, I'd rather play with my phone.

After much deliberation, the Committee restored one stanza to "butteless in the dim aurora of yet another alba."

When that fresh crop
of physicists lost their particle
accelerator, they went into
finance. Lucky us
the puffing guest speaker
nearly forgets to hold our
hand or am I being
derivative

Dante would have found a place for all the people who misap-
propriated his funds and those goons who made the soil toxic.
People we dare not name.

Beatrice would have picked up her second phone, screeching
you woulda coulda shoulda phoned it in. Dante would have been
found behind the bank with his face on it.

I admire the way you flaunt
your flautist fingers, the way you
assemble that sailor's delight
inside a bottle

Tonight may be the night
I trim my toenails
and tomorrow I shall rise
to have my hair cut

When you are just shy
of seventeen you are still effing
cold, I said to the weather
beside Robbie Burns

This is the best documentation on the subject but it lacks a
jouncing conveyance from another century when going for a ride
was beautiful and elegant innuendo.

The lyric demanded Robbie Burns, covering up the wheat and
bread given to the statues of Taras Shevchenko and the little girl.
It is our solemn custom to feed our symbols.

Yes, I am still making fugly mirrors out of safety sand.

Rumbles—
tummy of a yummy mummy
Tumbles—
here comes another one
Fumbles—
Forget about it, everyone makes
mistakes except for the kicker
right here
trying to extract a
lick of work
from the dead-letter office

He denies a smoke or spare change. Someone calls Orphée *asshole* (again). His huff is immortalized INSTANTER and his experience is written on every licence plate.

One time Goltz got away and scored a touchdown without the other Bombers and got in hot water for celebrating the song of himself. This is the Canadian version of the game.

Ineffable un-
smiling junk
shot

The Princess did not have to hunt very hard for images of Orphée. She found them everywhere, and then Orphée mansplained he was just finding them too. *Seriously.*

Her advice: plagiarize some paper about a nightingale or thrush and nab the preeminent MFA. Hope to one day advise students about sincere recognition of their prior learning.

Though his tasteful nudes pass muster, the Princess still has to answer to various boards and councils for the Arts.

Love gleaned early on
we would pass on the bridge
and not say hello

The Assiniboine is already
    broken up, little is lands of ice
evaporate

Orphée has a mild condition that is worse on Turtle Island, a dis-
order that turns everything into water under bridge. Your beautiful
face becomes like other beautiful faces.

In *Alice ou la dernière fugue*, Sylvia Kristel silently disrobes and
makes her descent. SPOILER ALERT: is she being sedated in
hospital or did she just crash into Köchel 491?

In the morning light, the surtitles explain that no one can re-
member what happened the night before. Orphée tends to blame
balls-out katabasis for his troubles.

Morse
Father of American
Geomancy
Patent the freshest molecule
that mixes it up
with this bad boy
Re: Morse
r we ok
r u mad @ me
texted every cock of the walk
once upon a time
on this freewheeling whirligig
or what I meant before
thumbing SEND was

— • — • —

Real people with real feelings emerge like phantoms from a begging bowl full of squashed mosquitoes. The Poet, motionless in his or her hugging machine, aches for relation.

The sweet flower of Cocteau's excitement pops up out of nowhere in sped-up frames. This is represented by a flower that withers in Cocteau's paws.

Elsewhere, VIA Rail wants to really stick it to the Princess.

Drip
the ecstatic soprano sang
in the key of David Hemming's boyhood
murdered by time

This is a literal translation of a Sapphic fragment found in a dusty old jug. We were under the impression that it had vanished forever.

The Princess is awfully confused by the copy-editing rules of our wretched world.

Sorry, how do you pronounce—
Sorrier, how do you pronounce—
Sorrier, sorry, what the—

The paper on Strangeness
and the paper on Sincerity
made a real difference

A squawk
of chicken talk
back of Sâkêwêwak
was all she wrote
till the surgically
altered lady sings

Really sorry, but how do you pronounce—

Someone will master the accurate pronunciation of a First People before Orphée reaches that *château* down below, if you get me.

Letters that allude to the papers just burst into flame. An othering of flaxen circumflexes was the result.

Jane Austen is to blame for all these meaningful silences.

Avasilichioaei
Moss of bossypants gloss
what happened years ago
when the Limerick
Junction was
immortalized or
amortized in a long poem
that perished instead of
knew how to publish
when Spring turned out
to be the worst promise
ever made on Yoga-
Suicide Bridge
Moss of bossypants gloss
or your loss, hoss

Years ago, a woman is still weeping over a poem taken down on a device in the wee hours. Years ago is a device like when Anacreon says, once again I seek a statutory no-no.

Once again, I slunk down to see the Princess, snubbing Love, scrubs away a plethora of daily chores.

Avasilichioaei contains a precise combination of vowels that open doors, even for the unedumacated. Yet upon the limbs of those vowels did we find the charm.

Head
hung low
ears pricked up
for the voice of
~~Robert Desnos~~ Cégeste
(or the voice of Jack Spicer attenuating his radio
 in Aquatic Park, listening to the scores, as if
 they could translate into CFL highlights)
Sex like awesome sauce wasn't the
point but it was an
honest mistake
honest

The Bard has twenty thrillion meanings for the word *honest*. Then whatever you can see in that ink/blot.

Everybody knows that Jack Spicer listens to baseball games through a magical horse. The magic of radio makes the poem contemporary. Jack Spicer is famous for his brief appearance in the movie *Vertigo*. They were both hated at first (sight).

Sex slathered in awesome sauce is still not the point. Honest.

Maybe you are the only
one to see the real me
along with other flannel
found in the machine

An upstart crow had flown away
with all our memories from the quay
although that day the SeaBus muster
stations meant nothing

They jumble up, these
masticated or hardened
hearts in sore need of
tenderizing

They respect my silence, announces the older poet, dying to tell
someone. He is first in line to get Orphée in trouble with the
Royal Canadian Mounted Police.

They (fondly) remember the time the Poet went missing. He was
sufficiently dishy and in a veritable state, according to the Raging
Métis Canoe Princess.

The Princess is not on the best of terms with this popular trade-
marked character.

A white-tailed hare (or 15, 16 of them)
curling up hareness upon a dark white backdrop
evokes that winter evening
is the only real thing from those parts
not as a memory of something that happened or a symbol or
anything
Ghosts (and cottontails) fall short somehow
needing you the way a door
cries like it needs WD-40
The illusory jackrabbit (or 15, 16 of them)
is up to speed on *The Visible and the
Invisible*, needing
no crutches
needing only snow in late April
the only real thing

Crutches are what the Poet uses on icy boulevards before the safety sand arrives. Barrels everywhere full of Foucault, Lacan, Žižek, Merleau-Ponty, and Truffletaff. Sometimes ice crystals in the air remind the jackrabbits they are more than handsome globes of snow.

Ghosts (and cottontails) never achieve this kind of reflection. They hop about beaten paths, thinking they are thinking. A white-tailed hare (or 15, 16 of them) can still reach the heart, some months after the fact.

Hooligan chinook
deep in mistaken brook
depleting fish talks
—Can you translate this poem into a more comfortable patois—
The eternal triangle
according to Palliser
where things disappear
—Can you translate even fishier versions of this fortified stock—
Listen to the drum
of another pronominal conundrum
petting sturgeon

A hooligan chinook is notable for its luminous jargon on ignitable evenings. Before sealing the deal, the Princess wonders aloud if Orphée is genuinely open to the odd bit of waterboarding. This is an example of a verbal contract. The water in the poem is full of all our usual crap.

The plumes of these neumes
have nothing on me, sister
whatever they sing

You still hit ENTER [or RETURN]
ain't that the truth
ENTER [or RETURN]
doing neither

Cégeste tells tall tales with the aid of stirring chironomic gestures.
"If I Could Turn Back Time" plays in a loop. It would cost an arm
and a leg to say more.

In *Get to Know Your Rabbit*, a marketing executive performs magic
until it becomes the business of making magic. This is some of
De Palma's finest work, missing only tarted-up art house flesh,
cut in half by split|screen Debussy.

I know what you did for the
whole summer, little suckhole
so produce a passable paper
that takes us somewhere

Now write it like a failed
novelist caught between a
lizard of a producer and a
despot of a director

That scene where body
doubles do the crocodile is
pretty far out
but what did it gross

The Poet does not know what is happening, and that is hard to
make a clean breast of. Suckholes are acolytes who save the dead
from stubbed toes.

According to Criterion, after wringing every last dreg of gumshoe
out of Raymond Chandler, Billy Wilder has a meltdown and trips
up the winner. Honesty is this hideous to behold.

Doing the crocodile is a surrealist gag, like bringing tomatoes
instead of roses to show your appreciation before finding only a
pool of tears where the crocodile was. Scissors! Tomatoes!

Alone at last, messages go
to zones we no longer visit ...

imagine each organ pump
over that terse auto-reply

fast-track the next cycle
quote Nietzsche or cummings

on the other side of the tracks
knee-deep into Fort Whyte

coming all over like it
never meant anything

even your famous humour
you little gonif no-mark

Fort Whyte is an idealized version of the past. It does not exist
in the poem but for a modest fee, you can snowshoe where the
buffalo roam.

Thanks to metempsychosis, Sammy Glick was soon slotted in to
be reborn at the top of the distribution racket. Based solely on
sales, Pythagoras figures that whoever straddles the gooey pyramid
has more Klout than Orphée.

No matter how crazy drunk in loneliness Philip Marlowe gets,
"gonif" is a slur he will never solve.

The significance of the circle is the circle
jerk
right behind an old-timey filter
Was it Godard who said the circle is evil
    or that in every film, a woman
    double-crosses a man
It is perfectly okay to want
to belong in the circle
for that belonging
to be captured
in our mouths
    full of wet hate

Pound totes could have stopped the Second World War.

The moment the meds
kick in
the illusory world dis-
appears

"We are all in the gutter
        but some of us
            are looking at the stars"

Out of nowhere
a bran new
depression
is declared

Orphée notifies the Princess that she burns like ice. After he runs
out of Petrarchan conceits, there is not much to say, or so she
says. Rip-off artist, muses the Princess, in spite of a truly stupid
pelvic response.

The citation is from a popular British soap, used right before a
husband and wife try to kill each other. A custody thing.

Even Golden Boy cannot wave his enchanted wheat over all these
boo-boos and kiss them better.

Ramp up
another 9/11
situ at one o'clock
cramped
with another ramp-up
another 9/11
the planes are just about to
nose the towers
speaking
metaphorically
out of corporate head-
quarters cheat-
sheet
things people say at work

A judge asks Orphée what his profession is, and the answer arrives in a mournful baritone. The Princess is uncontrollably tickled by the whole production. After all, Orphée is not the one on trial for feeling love, or for showing initiative.

Her witty remark about his lack of a pen smacks of the most seductive misandry. Meanwhile, Orphée wishes that life was more like a fugal sunflower in Varda's *Happiness*.

Delicate strains of
Spiegel im Spiegel
beat Hegel on a bagel
for fifteen buckaroos
(or is that Schlegel)
betray the contorted
guts of the prepared
piano full of butt-
plugs, echoing a
cappella of eighties
stumper, another
party in the Peg

The Princess has hidden people in her spare garret. A false note strikes latex and gives her/them away. Orphée is not the only one with performance anxiety.

Tabula Rasa grasses on her in the background but everybody is too busy studying the mirror within the mirror.

Schlegel is a baroque invention that the Poet owns.

Do you know so-and-so
extends the scratch-me-back
even when preoccupied
with plough, slough
and falling snow
slapped playfully for this
heap of
circumstances
twiddling glyph of
radio knob
wait what about me

Snowfall in May is not something you repeat in a poem, nor can it be proved, in poem or podcast. So much for Colorado low.

Had he his druthers, Heurtebise would insist on versifying Lux Winnipeg Limousine until the fumes were poetic plumes. Too bad he cooked his own goose before learning to really goose. It is no accident Orphée will soon go at the hands of cyberbullies.

Aglaonice awakens to a romance package for one in the Fort Garry Hotel, mere steps away from history.

CAUTION:
  SLIP
 TRIP
HAZARD
  UN
      LEVEL
           (L)ED
FLOOR

Despite relishing a hands-off managerial style, the Princess models a pair of monarch-eaten milkweed gloves before she removes the warning sign not far from McNally Robinson.

Eurydice slips then trips then hits her head on one of the red balls left behind by a Target store that is no more.

Orphée cannot decide whether they were ellipses or periods gone astray, but he would give up all of his well-hyped works to have produced only one of these balls.

Urlicht
a private kind of prayer
full of primeval light
so go stick it in the symphony
before the lyrical angel
hears throat-clearing
noises and glides over
takes a good long whiff
so go stick your oar in the
ethereal
this little portion of light
caught in supplement bottle
in an explosion of magnesium

A wardrobe malfunction reveals *L'Ange Heurtebise*. Work harder, sings the Princess. Stop reflecting! Swirling circus music means that a tabula rasa is being blown out of stuff the glass seller repossessed from Baudelaire. Har har.

The tabula rasa means we can start over like nothing ever happened anywhere before, not even turn-of-the-century boom.

The poke
is a joke
linked to that link
mere cycles ago
the study about love
abandoned by magic
in nine out of ten
homes named after
poets, their
jokes no longer
with us

Orphée is going to toss together a psychoanalytic study of the life and work of Cégeste so that Eurydice can keep a kicking baby more unbearable than himself. Glass peppers the music under them with barrels full of depressive tension.

A standing O. Designed by Robert Lepage, a giant romance package in the Fort Garry Hotel transforms into a sparkling tandem recumbent.

The popular peregrine falcon is now ready for her close-up.

BONES OF THE
LAST BISON*

---

*   Erasure of "The Last Bison" (1890) by Charles Mair.

wilderness,

rein   there

supple

Indian blood

gleamed

bespoke

wondrous

Degenerate

dissolved

plumed

rough   realm

aspens

open

I

Reverberate

leaves

tiny   simulat~~ed~~

lash~~ed~~

liquid

fulgent

Of

fading

prairies

idleness

silent

gadding   cry,

Saskatchewan   moan,

plain

Loneliness

undeflower~~ed~~

Pulsing

virgin

power

-bruised,

chuckling

clangour

Sorrow

swept

decay

warrior

faded

Nature,

relics

grassy   village

law

slopes

dusky

tasks,

howled

council

oratory

vanished!

encroaching

fiat,

no

love!

fled

-breed

tribes

vestiges

vertebrae

bones

Descended

Or

roamed

herds

Exhaustless

hoof

trod

waking

mutability

burst

vale

startled

covert

For

bison

eyes

form

drawn?
blood
trickled
Uneasily
loud
rent
no
flanks
again
congenial
survivor

frame!
that
awe
fell
neck
toss
head
wound
spirit
burned,
teeming
glamour
attitude
endowed

smokeless
sufferance
birth
freedom
Enough!
stupendous
primitive
loved
lived

loved
daily
wantonly
breed
herbage
sweet

greed

it

forbid

And, so

great

life

End~~ed~~

sordid

blast

regions

winter's

prairies

stood

wandering~~s~~

red

race

reckless

wanton

longings

grew

pale

terror

destruction

Strange

fire

enemies

hurtful

desire

The ministers

delight

waxed

men

yield~~s~~

yield~~ed~~

Meagre

shelter

To

stern

spoiler s

smokeless

sufferance

The

tender

length

revives

Too late,

failing
touch

kindred
shadows

Responsive
spirit

cities
rich

in

bare~~d~~

time

prairies

people~~d~~

perish~~ed~~

In solitude

vacant

once

earth

Wild   plain

savage nations   native wilds

now

grin~~ned~~

An awful anguish

gasp~~ings~~ deep

spasms
stride

defiance

Then sway~~ed~~   groan,

die~~d~~

SAFE
SPACES

1

admit difficulty
from the first, to conjure
forth abstract chums, tease wig-
wam out of thin air, for lack
of a better wampum
            to swap
                    that will withstand these
            tensions fair
                    & foul
academese a waft
                    of flax ablaze
or simile for madly smitten
blown into one of the
towns puffed up
with dust
            from the
                    valley
vedic alert bracelet
buried (alive?)
amid traces of safety sand
                            when <POP>
goes the culture (the bubbles
out) universal knock on
the doors of privilege, shrink-
wrapped & encased in plasticky
triplicate for our convenience
if not more ethereal than nodes
of our "friendship" since its
point of origin
                    when cognitive
tinkering went rogue with
baroque treatment
                    not to suffer
conversion into
                    entranced
                    euros gladly
where criteria find a niche
behind defunct barrel organ
passing window of maybe
one attent listener

                                        (less
                    pathétique than it
                                  sounds)
unless we are still open
for business, which begs
the question of our
celebrated correspondence
volumes of soiled laundry
                          twisting on a taut line
like marsyas flayed
for blowing double flute
as the next hyperbolic
analogy is demurely
suppressed
                    a nutritious part of
winning the war on
                          prosody
that soon heralds
rap of gloved fist
with little time to
                    slide tome
               after tome
          into big
          blue
          barrel

still terrified of that un-
prescribed, unscheduled
ejaculation
               [in a brontë book]
          well beyond the
perimeter of our
                    expectation
promptly fetishized
               with mouth on barrel
               with safety off
what subscriber
                    feeds
call a perfect storm
meaning grey, rain
unruly
          circumstance

then why not at this fateful tick of antique clock
the nightmare bathes in sweat
birth this baleful
                    exposition
    lonely swells
                of the soloist
shaved to greet the dark
with a customized chair
carried everywhere
why not for this dutiful crick
                        chill
                                limbs
                rep after
                        rep
the sound of sand in each
raised weight
                bony swells
                        of the soloist
impress with that memory
of biceps' beguiling
                plurality
grinding out
the sound of utter besottedness
                    boot
        sand
                under
                        flash memory
            booty
can now be removed
bathed in sweat
                from double
        exposition
rubber
        band to remember to switch
off wake up to
                plainchant or
                        stabat mater
or self-indulgent missive
to someone's mother
                    atremble

in a
            favourite
       chair
creaking everywhere
                        rep
            after
                        rep
fist-pumping digital mirror
why not [sic] minnow in ad
                        hoc cadenza
kicking sand into eyes
glued to exposed thighs
            lonely swells
            of the soloist
buried everywhere
engraved to MEET
                        THE DARK
fist-pumping cembalo forte piano
in chiaroscuro peep show
bathed in dread
counting the injured ticks
            seeds
                  unsown
or never known
   need
            more memory
like another hole in the head
filling in simile of wan
                        pail
when the recollection
            of so much
                              rain
      is merely lyrical cantabile
            rep
                  after
                        rep
upon rooftop
the nightmare adorns
lonely sweat
                  of the soloist
      worried
            everywhere

call to mind an occasion
when tintin lets you down
when tintinnabulations of
"bakhtinian carnivalesque"
(not to mention
                rings
within ethnohistory mug)
leave a tinny echo
              or a taste of tin
within your water
when you can barely
                 pick up
or proffer syllabus
keeping a close eye on
recontextualized carnal
appetites featured in
cleverly hidden
           pin-
         hole
spy in drywall
before bifurcation
praying to signifier
              of confused
          geese
feeling decidedly
deciduous
        sinking deeper
          into disturbed area
amid this diminuendo
of late summer creatures
waiting for that
modestly empowered
         woman of the poem
           (in clingy clobber)
to ride through the breach
        high
          above the saddle
             of shiny bicycle
to lean over the tracks
over one of the rivers

in one of the towns
                puffing hella good
                                spliff
        floating away from the haze
                    of yet another male gaze
flowing together
            here where we are so friendly
we may not murder one another
not even our frail characters
subject in every city
to affluent effluent
to that knockout
chloroform
            & other anxiety-
        inducing killers
            in creeping fabric
softener
            that evoke nature, the
woods, real lemons
                    proustian
flashbacks of things we
fear, things that disappear
unless we order now
to revive flagging
excitation
                however brutalist
in the shape of
                    grain
                commission
                building
mushrooming
over tax centre
                & campus
                dungeon
hurting brand
therefore re-
branded as
1940s computer
unbuttoning blouse
to take up a level
                    all this exotic
                    catfishing

another jet
   over head
drowns
     our faint
       good night
our armless winterreise
    another jet
drowns
out another loop of adolescent
slush, the forecast for freezing
   drizzle another
         goof
another gulf stream
    if we preserve brutalist eye-
sore
or relatively vacant jazzy
         haunt
another jet drowns
our flaunted convo with the music
prefect, perfect
     truth
     & reconciliation
re: galileo vis-
      à-
   vis
      tortuous inquisitors
maundering
   through copernican
       upset
another jet
fan shaming little
boy rooting for
     the wrong
  side, a
     worn copy of
winter journeys
    flips in north
wind
  to   -down text
  upside

novelty another jet drowns
in first class brand of
anguish
         via royal mail
lonely for two-spirit catch
or shattered ancestor
in that tattered good
               night
another jet
         drowns out
             perimeter loop
if we preserve this baggage
carousel
        dig ourselves
out of this deep good
night that steeps us
in stumps of winterreise
     another nonsensical convo
       skypeless in this brightness
       until another jet splits
in two,   us   truly
              clove/n
right along with our stupid
       good
          night
animal
     thumps
         in this slush, or
was that crunch, this
forecast for missing
what is not there
         awfully

that mad ache for archival
saliva does not quite revive
the page-turner
            from last
night, helping to refresh the
piano quartet in a
              minor
chided lovingly for her debut
performance
            ah, but let us be true
to these leavings, not a crumb
out of place
   or remember when
                   "the baroness"
von freitag, etc. sd/ several true things
in the old days /driven
            nuts
by the whole
            stink of artifice
let us stick leaf to scrapbook
then rewind spool like krapp
unless we step out
              unbondable
       lovely
into rough
         around the edges
nocturne, some chopinesque
colour
       or tonal refraction
of those dudes nervous
about furtive sips of
beer on the bus
             still on watch for
riparian surprises
shored up
        before the river freezes
before the pipes
are kaputski

let us jot
    down
         grandisonant
is the oed word of the day
but where to stuff all this stuff
perhaps in a skit where love is
hidden
    behind a murphy bed
featuring memory foam
though even on the ride home
the poem was finding form
         craning
     to admire
    its own
excellence, an
     aphrodite
kallipygos in her own right
totes the image of the age
so rather than move the
furniture around
let us arrange
    picnic banquet
[for one] until that selfie is
spot on
    [wine-dark silk]
     with no comment
with little recommendation
except another
    slag
   heap
in the works, tightly
compressed into
belated valentine
fashioned out of
this unfinished
vinteuil gew-
gaw
   still jawing
     in men's room
murmuring of mozart
mahler, wolf, etc.

still in reverie over that
soprano with green hair
breathing romanticism
blissfully rinsing hands
of recognition of a poet
because in a weird way
this town is perpetual
festival
        filled
                with absence

door to door, our
constant, our delicious safe-
word is recession, the gift of
always being in one, no

          non-

             con-

sensual outbreaks,   desire
or old-timey oats
       beaten down by flaps of apathy
the constraint our meta-
data reshuffled in outmoded
        struct {
            to strut
            each stutter
       }
    of memory
        each pointer to nil
in forgotten days, a shade
gamey to the true gamer
infrastructure the hack
we want to
          project
        tag
          & flag
with detectors, chiefly as
deterrent to the idea,   desire
in stretch of unisex material
emerging from hybrid

            con-

tempt, our delectable

           safe-

word is suppression
no one in the accident
hurt, only barrels of

          sand

real as you & me, a
symbol for pointer to

           null

        another sex

thing

between us
        (or lack of one)
codified
        server-side
                if only to con-
form with epidemic
beaten down by mud
                flaps
or whatever they put in
        flapjacks seeping
                into sleeping flesh
each lyrical outbreak
                a type of stymy
in this sty
        thinky plagues
                        con-
signed by our officials
with repossessed think-
tanks
each lyrical beast
        faint morse for
        radioactivity scene
        in chinese roulette
    the constraint
rolling over freedom
of other tongues, only not
here please
door to door, a
knock before this cata-
strophic
            con-
solation prize, the
gunrunner's
aesthetic
come full
            circle
        (jerk)
bam!

if snowy prairie street, the
hereafter is redundancy
just waiting to happen
if just for once
                concern your-
self with growing concerns
funny in prison camp, to
dig deep then emerge
with
        l'atrophie
                du moi
while single citizens pine
for trolley bus(s)es or beer
parlours gone parkade
in the name of progress
we particularize the
            times change(d)
            high & lonesome
            club
                & its {culture
            not condos} branch
            of semiotics:
                            read
        now we are strata
of the down
            & out
still aching to hear
erratic benediction
of a fading genius
thrice an outsider
now, kill, kill, kill
hours in the library
thrill, conjure forth
reconstructed horns
of warning for have-
not harshness
while purgatorio
can wait
            at will call

sandbagged against
recession, being in
  recession for near
    eternity, just until
you get back on your
feet, this music will
render heaven
hoity-toity
extravagance
            in the nose-
  bleeds
        if a light rain
for good measure
in terms of mytho-
poeic bullshit, echoes
of shepherd horn
      more mournful
waiting for loverly
assistance, snugly
nestled between
     scherzi,   safe as
houses half the price
as back "home"
           denoted by
         lugubrious tuba
shaking up the tempo
               bar
               by bar
    to flesh out
    forever the
    prophet of
    our sorry
        times, yeah
   sorry, sorry

retro as poly-
gonal render in obsolete
                        z-
buffer every point of light
accountable as disposable
peel here
good old world monkeys
with opposable thumbs
dumbing
            down
                quick
on the trigger
            EMOTE
prides self for insane
                    reaction
                time
        a mote
                in dusky
                        noir
over shot
    after shot
        the high score
must help
    against the enemy
being everywhere
        triggers
                nostalgia
for mindbender
    for posable action
for every point of fright
before propaganda
        got so through the roof
in discount
            bin
beside decapitated
beauties
        on cover
                shots

beside impulse
items, points
   card, the
numbing of
   nerve
 endings
each execution
   a win-
win caught on new
phone with golly
or gosh concise
commentary
hears a sudden noise
the size of a varmint
& reaches
   for heirloom
lines up 'nucks
   in a row
fires over
  violation, broken
accord
  a polyphony
    of polygamists
shoots boys out of
   mystical town
the price of perfect order
   has gone through the roof
gosh or golly
   gum-
    drops
with free automatic
ingenuous aw shucks
'tude
 if you buy right now
our right
  to bare harms
in the buff with
   both
   barrels
less efficient
than scattershot

cartoonish critters
in conjunction
  with splatterfest
musky the real man
trigger
      warning
          trauma album
does it
      because he loves us
like a flag
draped over
      pendulous
                junk
or gonadic
          disasters
in the sun
  in the love/sick
                    dawn

beyond neuro/logical quirk
calculated within quark
on miraculous device the
size of calculus caught
in the nick of sublime
beyond grainy simulation
incredible chemistry on
slide, crude feeling
meticulously dis-
           sected:
sound of train
behooves each
depression such
thingummies contrite
from the root
    crushed to   *pieces*
    bruised   *crumbled*
    worn   *away*
whittle down
mystery, condensation
more grist for mill
posit
      eloquence is *heard*;   poetry is
                    *over*heard
erotic rarities
avoid valuation
      relentless through the night
   with grain wanted elsewhere
with this controlled burn
externalized on the cheapest of post-
consumer pap, aping gem-encrusted
cover to lure out of hiding ornate
lapidaries, outbid by
tender proclamation
of vellum
       that pathology will suffice
       that deviation will show a

surplus of pluck
this quarter, going
through a sticky patch
being our own best
interest to slash splices, perhaps
have both narratives

                  removed

have the whole
family tested for
       inexecrable gene
then brood a while longer
over another bridge that
needs building, between us
                beneath taut horsehair
at back of mouth
that misuse of *concrete*
in leaden hands, in
prairie casino, rolling
heady concoction of
hello serotonin soaked
through with tweaked
pheromones as if
glutenless glutamate
could make you
         ~~dopa~~mine
the one & only pleasure
to ever sashay past
             "suicide bridge"
& live, chopping
wood for flames
sheerly to drag
volumes out of dickensian
scuttle
      in cultural imperative
with imperialist game
face throwing up   tomes
like the famed whale
that was never whaled
presumably beached
or driven out by the

price of one bedroom
nesting papered over
when it could be said

    i feel for you

nope, not even the scan
can capture this unseen
                rush
no trace other than
spinal spiral
      down-
    ward   unless the ward
is also feeling the
        pinch,   WAKE UP

mellow out calmative
on back of curriculum
vitae ill-treated by
        toner
running out of tone-
        down
     time-
   out
window for yellow mug
of bright tomorrows
something about the marrow
or intestines
       plucked out
sworn to be gospel
      on testes
meaning normative
     like you
       & me
the mail-order boner
homeless, not even
perking up margins
      of a molten
   core
  moving through fields of
yarrow
    unsung *achillea*
      around bright
sunflowers
   in *le*
     bonheur
our post-office affair
spineless, not even
time for sallow morning
afterthoughts
      pulling off
to unlikely animality
or a cornucopia of

unicorn hypotheses
　　schadenfreude is magic
　　our intellect trucked out
for cross-border outfit
gasping at smog
　　　　like never before
yelling over ablative
on back of *currículo*
schematic
　　moving through fenced
articles
　　frantic to find
　　　　　profit
　　motive
home on the free range
once again on the hunt
in guilt-free rave
　　　running out of
　　　　　minutes, life
time for mallow hug of
condescension
　　　to parrot
ally/ship for the oppressed
organic
　　greening
　　　like you
　　　　& me
　　　still haunting
　　　that site of
　　　speculum
blunders
　　plugged
　　　as wonders

by this grey light
upon dusty table
more ink on scrap
refurbishes happen-
stance, the talk on
interiority total
no shows, or
tweet coined
"tumbleweeders"
avidly clicking
interested, or
evoke cool, swell
thicket, denuded
of sounds, foliage
thick associations
steep in white cup:
        gulp of
           gular pouch
    stuffed with
indigestible
      oneiric
        inklings
upon panes   a
mayfly on last
day on planet
half in love
with easeful
    fluorescents
where frond
    after frond
affection blooms

     >nabokovian
        obsession for
           blues<

for each monarch
   & fritillary
      with proboscis

deep into meadow
        blazingstar
soon sucked dry
            at edge
    of wetland
to accompany
    schubertian ear-
worm, case of shack-
wackiness warping
concept of slippage
    in clawfoot time
to scrub white/brown
body
    leaping
            in sleep
stuck at lectern
turning on students
        who long for the coast
        for the wobbly ocean
while we catch global
broadcast, crave those

    soft   white   silences

scatterings of sand

forget those gullets full
of slime, water, anything
but what they most crave

            (if only this
            tight cocoon
            would bust!)

a trick of grey light
today upon dark
                eyes
that deems life
potable
            only the festival
                cup did not live
                for very long

garrulous with lust the gaze
at excellent spectacles
stockings, the whole package
buried beneath a fresh layer
of sand, the body blue
as dead common barrel
unless there is one hour to be
mortified, taming
                    danger of the
object of costly
          ubi caritas et amor
behind glass
                    perilous with must
for allergic goal-oriented
goody goody
attached to glossy pectorals
a kind of sand-kicking
damnation
                    the whole wreckage
buried beneath a fresh cluster
of zebra mussels
                    lost in the haze
of a chinese picture
                    at cannes
          unless there is one hour to be
rectified by cordial chat
          with this chit
                         of a thing
wearing thin
               like mesh traps
or the provocation of stockings
hurried beneath suspected crush
leaving
          sand, the body blue
as beached whale
                    & then
some, range of the

human voice bled
behind glass
                    adulterous with
grist, shifting
     on sacks of grain
          a prairie narrative
of verboten strokes
on dead farms
for acerbic cold-blooded
moods
          phasing out
former sites of plain-
spoken
          destruction
                         a looks-
     good-on-paper approach
covetous
          & beyond
reproach

accrete or
decommission
DEFCON
emission or
savage clap
of calumny
like foul wind
in
   valleyed
         inversion
feminine
essentialism
in the face of
new-fangled or
déclassé effort
controlled by
colourful
   toxi/city
        hey kids
     leap
        onto leaf
           pile
before it is mowed
down to prevent
mould, sticky
that smouldering
glare, eyes
water, tear
in foul wind
heart races
to emergency
fight or flight
phos(phite or
phate) surprise
torn down to
erect innovative
heap/sex site or

condo/strip
mall combo
if so sale of
matriarchal
archetype
is final, no
wrong idea
of the thing
itself, just
acute
  accent
on the verge
of vanishing
varnishing
table for
company, a
pair of eyes
to peruse
recycled
discourse
reinforce
ban on
urbanity
saturate
micro-
economy by
deadline
with festive
ribbon or
scandalous
crime tape

DO NOT
CROSS

deadly
serious
detritus

isn't it geomantic
    this recombinant last
kick at the can
   in narrow pool
the well dried up, the
flowers for food withered, the
heroes of the zeroes
defamed, flamed
forgotten like that password
recombination
unless tonight you fancy geomancy
    this last lick
        at dehiscence
the swell cried out, the
roots for food tainted, the
spurious of the prurient
deflowered, flambéed
forgotten like those meds
recombination
unless mantis sex novelty
card was a joke
we're in the mood for geomancy
more pricks than kicks
at acupuncture last week
the last knell pried open
    DENIED, the
limbs for food crunchy, the
slaver of exquisite cadavers
deformed, flummoxed
forgotten like that other thing
recombination
unless your trance poem
was faking geomancy
because out of bucks
sucks monkey balls
    in a wheelbarrow
the content ruined, the

fodder for food fallen
victim to a cleanse, the
prescription of the post-neo-
something sculpture
   site of
        rupture
      (or fracture)
       deboned, fluted
forgotten like that
              can(n)on
in the place of dirty looks
recombination
              spouting off
   in tongues
unless you mean
          geomancy

tonight it feels good to stretch out
hack a wide swath
the height
& depth
     of one's positionality
fear amid makeshift *feria*
lost in funny mirror
lapping at root
where
    the land's sharp
    features seemed to be
    the century's corpse
          outleant
     calling to mind
     that lovely picture
     in our naked copse
     that haunted look
     boggles, stymies
     frustrates, eggs
     on preoccupation
     for wage slaves
     on injury leave
eager
to spin
    tires of a holistic courier
fleet-footed along FLEET, popping
          wheelie over
        railroad ties
    beyond NO
        TRESPASSING sign
onto
    BRÉBEUF
       [slaving over
        savage grammar when the
        unpoxable attacked, though
        he was the only one to be
        beatified for his pains]

before
    disappearance   through leafy wall
    beside disturbed area
        the place where clouded
        sulphurs & painted
            ladies are in clover
stellar listeners
for tales of
wanderlust
strewn across path
resonance with right-
wing media feed
blotch shots of
famous shrug
raw sewage
into river
rushed off feet
yet too slow to snap-
chat or find time
for the prelude
    & fugue in a
        minor
or if you have more
minutes how about
              the first
    train:
        tender girl song

whoa
    the tonal
        of the self is an island
          suffocated by sea cucumber
farms
    where even our easy-to-
        sharpen invective
    arrives
          DEFECTIVE
doused in abstract
preservatives
       where the mouth
of discount giant
        makes greeter
zombies of us all
    suffocated by bran new
chemical fumes
      whoa
         even our tease
of social intervention
        regresses
back to choke sex
& other forms of
      ownership
beneath brilliant cave
        paintings
a halcyon whiff
     of peon
    everywhere
just not dinner table
       talk
        each moan
of the self is a spiritual
mountain where coffee
        is picked
by uniform
   hands
but we digress
     from our general

protest
        tenderly educated by cucumber
            entry
                forms
life with region two compatibility
our favourite elective
                    roused by traction
when the junket
        becomes a matter of self-
preservation
                on that heap of
uncounted
                consumer
power points never to be
fully exercised
                    mimicking slam
dunk
        yes you have to be firm
            but not even that bran new
                            superdong
can save you, or do a
frigging thing
                best not to
mouth off
            about mounting
            micro-
        aggression
            suffocated by fermi
paradox or plot about
android tricked
into clone
            labour
& other forms of
                ownership
whoa
        cucumbers
                our ghouls never to be
        fully
            exorcised

will our snowy corridor
corydon meet aesthetic
criteria or too kitsch
hive/mind for our
violent buzz buzz
relays of box office
totalitarian allegory
subdue, subsume
high octane hand-
maid explosions
empower detached
bungalow dormer to
crawl back into itself
another one in the
eye for celebrity
spectacle trash
breeding heartfelt
aspiration to sex [tape?]
        or tall tabloid tale
wagging in this
          fierce wind
in the future
      revolving box
set storylines will self-
destruct before ad-
diction can occur
sophocles turns
in no man's land
hooked on our
patriarchal
      (oedipal?)
trilogies where fatherly
love is reinforced by
vaguely ethnic attacks
or alien motherships
anything to quash
autonomy in the

individual spirit
preferably with
rapid-fire chase
sequences &
repression of
heathen desires
subbed by sub-
lime sublimation
will see you now
with surcharge for
disappointed face
texts manufacture
issue even when
the emoji is up
when snap
    chat snap
momentum
trading gets
supersketchy
only the snip
snip of a hair-
dresser,   verse
            on the floor
illuminated by
that inner light
icy walks, the
barrel not yet
used

lost for that flicker
    of a premonition
in such vacuous
      gorgeousness
the anguish of these contorted
quixotics
     loses its place
cackling softly in the
         accidental
where there is no need
to invent the voice
    of a lovely entity
our continuous present
far from the lugubrious
       gloom
of half-forgotten
      islands
oblique histories
    of shadowy
        conquest
that soundly upbraid
    our ancestral lethargy
  lust
    for that flicker
of a candlefish
      in such vacuous
        gorgeousness
the squish of these torturous
sonics
    produces space
that aches craftily in the
      accidental
where there is no need
to invent the notion
    of vanishing tongues
our monotonous reality
    far from the lugubrious

gloom
     of toxic inversions
in the
     valley
        of the shadow
of estranged methodology
interrogation
        of ancestral languor
           lost for that flicker
             of a perversion
        in such vacuous
          gorgeousness
the anxiety of this mortified
eroticism
     hides its face
hacks softly in the
       accidental
where there is no need
to tear
     animals
   & birds
from our bare
      bodies
        trash icons
       torch chattel
behind bypasses
   under bridges
deep
  within
    underground arteries
   pawn the
      entire
        load
for that flicker
     of a promise
in such vacuous
     gorgeousness
no, there is
    no need

solidarité
found poem overlap
with greatly anticipated

EXPLOSION

black friday deals
with just a click
from the security
of your home/or
nomadic hovel /\
in a freaking heart-
beat you can rent
to own this poem
save a trending
meme today
rated N for NO
ONE
      on the back of
bus stop perception
ad training for natives
for steinbach syrians
soon we will all be
one book one nation
checking every book
every blue barrel
from noon till night
if we can have a whip
round, afford cronies
endless inquiries, slush
fund plebiscites, art
in all the bureaucratic
washrooms of the world
          non-consensual
          non-contractual
        fantasy of that
black friday halter
dress subject to

the blackest black
friday violence on
record,   now
                available
            in ear-
        drum-bursting
            blu-ray gift set
potable reserve
water not included
with free shipping
in surplus ideology
where environmental
terrorism beggars
belief amid
            transcendental attacks
from within
we can see every drop
of the destruction from
our glass house in
1960s dick fantasy
of global warming
where we ache for
cold architecture

            in a quiet little town
            not far from here

bootstrap kick-
starter campaign
for our conscience
if that were not
so widely banned
on campus too
but at the first sign
of abnorm brewing
it was like a black
friday movie if
not the finale
of the farewell
symphony

       shoot
           in all directions
                  attack
enthusiast nearly whacked
by jacked-up tot
staunch believer in boot-
leg cache holstered
in bra or butt
in all the ecstasy
there was an outpouring
of unprecedented feeling
a dramatic footnote
for our formalist group
hug
       brackish the nuisance hack
for crackhead guardian
bleeding from paunch
really putting the "arse"
in arsenal
in all the ecstasy
there was a moratorium
on unlicensed concern
traumatic marginalia
for our formalist
           safety
         check
        smack enthusiast nearly
plugged by huggable brat
peacemaker strapped
     to clavicle or clavier
in all the errata
there was a soaring
    of recent
         RATATATTATs
semi-automatic
      automatism
for our formalist trust
              fall

splat the endocrine
             of evolution award
     or launch fail
anger bolstered
        by click
          or cock
in all the egregiousness
there was a
              stockpile
of collectible death(s)
a phlegmatic
           gasp
for our formalist flash
mob
      spell/checking plaque
for lacquered liquor
lover with raunchy stash
blasting mall
             rats
in muggerly
        give as good
              as one
        gets

land-
  slide land-
fill monday   ton(ne)s
of black bags crammed
with outdated devices
countless gizmos the
wrong colour galleries of
monetized violence with
bright bulletproof
  blankets /for kids\
        the loss leader
sides of subprime slime in discount bin
budding buddy bromcoms about credit
default swap the woman who went
public on the
cover of *fortune* on the
        cutting room floor for the
feel good little guys who bet on the
misfortune of others
        & SCORED
bigtime liking those
odds apocalyptic gamble
the maturity of our security
odds for 57 metaphorical
hornets buzz in brain
stave off blood from
trigger-finger triggers
on a fresh sugar rush
riding the curve of
migraine forecast
the worst time of year
for chronic repression
when bearded angels
full of facialized spunk
raise flaming swords
unite to save themselves
from temptation of the

female of the species
with an outbreak
of high fives a rash
of random blasts
mow down the part
that offends with the
right to own choice
ton(ne)s of black bags
say it with hallmark
network special
the host demos
teflon blankets
another pox upon
us fire when ready
we are just having
a moment here
this carpool rage
this commute to
the afterlife is an
abominable bitch
the whole climate
deal scientific crap-
              shoot
           first dispatch
drone later
    while the
night is still young
really any belief
can be militarized
whatever
gets you off
extirpated from
jumbo cup too hot
running out of
safety sand in
analogy no longer
trending aggregate
of jaw droppers
but yes we can
pop the new pill

from upstart medical
dot- com yes we can
fix neighbourly strife
communal dysfunction
gubernatorial crackpots
with oil industry junk
shots with sanctimonious
scenes of familial bondage
with accidental
judgments & casual s-
laughter on a bigger screen
around the throat of an
albatross underdog
at the base
salary
          of the great orgy

let us compare
geographies as emblems
of manifest destiny
a flutter of mud-
puddlers attached
to unforsaken wasteland
a gaggle of geese
      honk optimism
in misguided
          sevens
            let us
              spare
monogamy as emblem
of manuscript density
      a clutter of sod-
turners attached
  to naked ambition
    a glide of trumpeters
        honk optimism
over modified
      lettuce
        just a
           snare
mythologies as emblems
manufacture dastardism
schmutters from schmatta
industry gleaners attached
to storied embroidery
a giggle of ganders
      honk optimism
in mortified
    formation
      let us
        stare
monopolies in the emblem
of manipulated anxiety
an attack of mood

addict attached
  to spent adrenals
  a boggle of neurons
 fire feels
into overloaded
   sectors
      LET US
       WEAR
bare-assed misanthropy as emblem
of scripted identity
shield our terror
with modesty's cloak
do food, sleep
sex, occupational
swamp
   working
for our personal
panopticon
without a scrip
or waiver or
   safe-
 word

another redux in flux
meet me on confusion
                    corner
at the height of fresh
craze
        flanked by dominant
cultural argot   the tragic
collapse of our circle
jerk
        brutalist communal
hangout
        our supreme meme
            loogies
commas
        exclamation
                    points
within virgin
inches
        trumpet forth
more sand
then tentatively
                sap
rows of veiled
                faith-
            bombs
blasphemy
            claws
with sexy
    secular
    epiphanies
then
        STOP to admire white-
    breasted
                nut-
        hatch
acrobatics
        before the

blast
　　grosses only
a few mill
converted into
revolving ticker
　　　　　　47 beheadings the
　　　　　barter of conscience
but one day
real brutalism
will be recognized
for its anxiety
of influence
　　　　　paint
in sonnet
falling
　　　drip
　　drip
　　　drip
into sculptor's
eyes
　　　that behold
subversion of
pilaster
　　　deliberation
in rupture
　of pediment
walls throbbing
with unspoken
talk
　　touching
　　　　　on the
erotic
　　　in flap of old-
school mantle
　　　　　flagging
action that hurt
　our brand
mimetic the balletic
swivel to please
　　　　old-

boy backer
visceral blobs
                must

vacate by
nightfall
subject to psycho-
analysis on
        fainting couch
a concise
        [yet fractured]
        history of art
                a
discipline of mannerly
mannerism
stretched out onto
refined madness
or many-minded
oracular outbursts
smashing pediment
in the only chain
in town
        our bare feet
bedecked with ore
tread of grimy faces
our painted
mouths
        full of
                cake

piece together
  pasticcio,   our revival
              ripped to
     shreds
           once homage
to one's comrades
presages foul dish
or pastiche
in the pejorative
spat out
in the figurative
reborn like inmate in block
             of marble
rousing desire in
    ribald tapestry
             ripped
to shreds
on multiple choice
say, by papal land concerns
    the size of a symbolic fish
in presentation on
meaningful
       objects
the glossary from
       flânerie
           to *fétiche*
or *glaucous*
      to *glock/en/spiel*
ripped to
       shreds
in celestial fury
slow to show
in certain
doctrines
tears that formulate
intricate dress
in objectified re:
production
      once images
for the age

                    suffering ages
of rejection
till we are
reborn like inmates in blocks
                    of marble
with the scent of
censorship codes
                from
        parrhasius
                to *petronius*
since impotence
cures
        are no tonic for our
architectonic iron
works
                    so please leave
        all *dionysian*
                    to *dystopian*
        ur-demi-
                urges
                    at the door
marked by frustrated
motives
            refabbed
                    as ornaments
along with versified
contortions
            of sheer
connotation
                    ripped to
        shreds
            no more
philosophizing
        the joys of pessimism
set to
        lovelorn
                    chord
elbow
    to elbow
            with one's comrades
prefigures piping
reheated *pasticcio*
the size of a hyperbolic gash

historically the fashion
in presentation on
recontextualized
                              space
from *pillar*
                    to *post-*
                         post-
                    post-
fragmentary
                    gloss
caught in
                    elongated throat
our schematic
ripped to
                    shreds
rousing
              desire
in
     mistaken
                    installation
piece
          so please help
whoever knocks
                at the door
[in theory]
                    once *frémissement*
                              to fromage
we could appreciate
before depreciation
of the cosmetic
metrics
              of this
                         pesticide, or
ready-made
                    blue
                    barrel
overturned
each
         granule
                         a
pastiche of
              morally
bankrupt
instances

IDEAS
OF
NORTH

baton
—rise
crash down once more
flush on the hairline
of this rocky border
town

Slow to a
crawl

The pit
gapes open,   invites you to unearth
inorganic
solids
that problematize our means, a
panel discussion on prairie
surrealism
where
living skies
& artificial lake
drown out
drowning voices
even a primitive mask that is part violin
even a pressure that is brain-
eating amoeba
in some
unchlorinated
backwater

Wait!
—the object looms, dark
& formidable
They've been bear-
baiting with
chum
again

why not recall how the public square floods
                                    with light
                                          & heat
            amid mortal selvage, the magisterial
                        example of found litanies
fatidic inklings, plaster
            paws
                  clutching the
                        VOID

                        —that anthropomorphic look
                        gives way to metamorphic chunk
                        of churning love, polymer
                              & fluorescent admiration in the
                                    lyrical possibilities of circular form
                                    restless arcs that strain their
            boundaries
                  with fragmentary shapes
                        & abruptly interrupted energies
all the way back to Stella's
                  Saskatoon Series
            caught
                  in the light unevenly
                        render language in the light
                              desire in the light repeatedly
                  those thighs those teeth those parts in the light
                        kisses in the orchata in the light repeatedly
            gloss over unrestrained delight in the light
                  strange blazon in the light yes in the
                                                light

2

Now let it settle
a bit in the middle. Let them work out
which outfit was which. Meanwhile, a poetic
flim-flam man steals
                    into Flin Flon
evades detection
with only one thing
in mind
              in the light
          rhombs
                  fall in the light everything
          for that head in the light that head-
          dress in the light
          turns into trapezoid or primitive
          strains straining in the light the rain
          becomes clear quietude in the light
          those parts wait for hands in the light
          those hands open like birds over-
          head in the light
                        a staircase a
                                  horse half a
                                            face

—passing time in touristy bliss, perusing whatever
in the dime novel persuaded Creighton to name the
other side after Flintabbatey Flonatin, or so the
ballad goes
              his reputation as a ladies' man, his prosperous
              bacon & cheese concern, his
                                    descent
                    down to Lake
                                Avernus
                    packed inside
                                an iron
                                      pike
              down to Esnesnon
              the sunless city

where everybody
is ass
backwards
& stones are too plentiful
to be worth a second look
merely what can be
extracted from them

missing prolegomena
for next manifesto, wordless on the
unspeakable subject of
snow
in summer, nodding
off to shin-bang
treasured oddity, once
coveted bumber-
shoot blossom for a winsome
merchant of four seasons
caught fondling
columns
of a dead bank
façade
patrons
of that portrait
of the poet
ornate
blade
bound
by orchid
stabbing
staticky
backdrop
for a hint
of fur

3

Here
we forget which side we are on
until our claim seems
meaningless
if not legless
gliding like osprey
over uncongested road
when a music
emerges from nearby, maybe the clink-
clank of Nibelungs
ruining their lungs
to pluck that stuff
out of orchestral
depths

wave at the repetition of words
flesh passing us by
hair that whips in the wind
benumbs our fortitude
wind that erodes our whims to root to bone
to the end of time, or anything
on a frolic of its own

wave at the repetition of faint portents
motivated by the most stellar minerals
wave at the instant that is not an instant
when that face ... ah, who can tell
how cold it is, away from that heat
away from that heart
when those feet leave without a sound

—freshly fixed at Hair
on the Rocks, there is
another attack of self-doubt
while climbing
the
100
stairs

for a better vantage
point of the storm
                          sewers
thinking such precarious
                              notions have gone to
pieces, tactility in a dark
            theatre is not nothing, our finest analogy
was just torn up in
                      delusional harbour
where beetles have
              stopped at the belt of an elm
thinking
            that would be the easy way
                          out, a ladder in a Miró
where a mossy green
has nothing to do with black
spruce, the envy of outlanders
eager to lay mitts on these
                          ore
                      samples
reckon their percentage
of copper, zinc
              & fools' gold
until the whole
              thing goes
                      bear-shaped

4

It may not be the
Eiffel Tower but
we
like
the
smoke-
stack
that used
to make
us sick
& dirty
our laundry
 silently
  bear the scars
   of a molten life
  flowing
   down
to disclose the curve
of that carnal space, lost in pointed
shoes upon ashen girder-like passenger
in Underground Fantasy *in silver panel that feigns*
being fresco
  at the foot of Fra Angelico
fending off shades
of protest, slashes
 of Tyvek
   echoes of opera in a veiled quadrant
   that is sparkling piano leg
no, scratched woodcut
   of lonely strangers

better yet, the first Camberwell
Beauty with antifreeze in its
    veins
impeccable emblem for an
    Idea
     of North

that ominous doomer
who hibernates at least
twice a year to
conserve
    moisture

        Pangs! You clean up nice & boast
        such a likeness to love the
        plot is lost
            & everything is
            weak-kneed equilibrium

        O pangs
            in that forbidden pelt
        you create such brute confusion
        husking
            eyes, voice, face,
                hands, hair, teeth ...

then one day we get THE
CALL, a curt voice asking
us to please come
collect our books
because the mine
        is nearly kaput
& local interest
    is scheduled for the chop

                BEASTIE
                  FOR
                COUNCIL

reanimated by that acrylic
rendering of a man
      in mauve
   netting
      several more
         suckers

5

As verification of our identity
    & assertion of our faith
        in our national heritage
why not take the
      plunge
        & leap
            into lime-
              stone
                abyss
    only what if we fail
    to systemize or monetize the
    currency of these raw hurts

    only what if there is a bird
    where a beautiful head

      ought to

    be, scratching blotches
    that have no interpreter

lacking the few adjustments
required to become a hero
of consciousness, to dwell
on how wonderfully
we cleave
      to notice straight off the bat
the nudes
    descending
      staircase
are not even ready

      We have company
      so let us agree to disagree
      everything is so fracking
      precious
    we positively ache to etch
    epigrams
      in pumice

or however ignorant
of igneous
              spray our names
              & prideful declarations
              on Precambrian
                            Shield
          to somehow burnish
          those billions of years
          with our digital
                    reflections

6

Listen, the ice
            is *breaking*
      terribly
            brittle   it rustles
                  like dresses in period novels
      cracks   up
around red-
      necked
            grebe
                  beside the dock
                        in The Pas
roused from nightmare
about Clearwater
                  "itch"
                        to capture the most
                        darling Indians for
                        our menagerie
if we could just get the
Kwakwaka'wakw
in the Kikiwak Inn
ixnaying meal tax
with treaty number
                        where the women come
                        & go, giggling over that
                              flirt who wants a gig
                                    in the kitchen
where
      I see my life go drifting like a river ...

            halting in the middle
            of the Saskatchewan
            touched by the tale
            of two labourers
            who died
                  building that bridge
between old
      & new Cree
            Nation

Over dinner, we are at our leisure
to solve the world's problems
to express ourselves
            about Betty, Native
urchins
            in makeshift churches
            set up in railway towns, the
                        flames licking
                        closer to tar sand
                        Götterdämmerung
forgetful of the muskrat
amid Compton's Tortoise-
shell, shelter
            to a ladybird
on account of wind
chill factor, reverberations perched
like ravens outside our
            window, the verve of our lazy
            vernacular, the colour of coral
in the gut of a carp, that shock
of hair if only the beloved
would grasp that hint
of lightning
            that long search for wet
                        metal
deemed mental
by commentary
            uneasy near panicky upon cold bench
            in the square as empty as eternity
            yes, in the square as empty as eternity
            where sleep is not fitful
            where heretic temples make no sense
            nor these jerky migratory motions
            talking in grandiloquent yawns
            flat the demeanour of this ardour
            that stabilizes
            like a blip roaring behind a cloud
            ignoring gerundial anything

 —the subject does not arise
     that for generations, we have taken
        Greyhound
            have emptied
                our pockets
    of every loose
        nickel
have been swept
      in the
        shape
          of a T
for errant
     implements
         (one Indigenous
       woman finds the whole
      process degrading, her de-
     capitating heyday
    well behind her, the other
    ladies laughing at the idea
      of having their butts
        fully checked out)
before riding through the night
    with large
    boxes full
    of cereal
         eyes half-
     open
       at primordial
         dawn

7

We subsist at a key so low
the music of the wood
frogs
  beckons us back
     with a din
    like quibbling
   ducks
that drives
the usual croakers
     out to the road
just to be heard
like little green tenors
 mimicking Vickers:
     Dem Land, das Tristan meint,
     der Sonne Licht nicht scheint:
     es ist das dunkel
     nächt'ge Land,
     daraus die Mutter
     mich entsandt
     als, den im Tode
     sie empfangen ...
just the trick to hood-
wink listeners
  even choirmaster
    & missus
tracking the tones
in every poem

    Next stop
    Carnegie Hall!

the reception
is incredible
& for once
   no one asks
     where ideas
     come from

far more vital
precepts spring
            to mind
in the presence
of the new arrival
from South Africa
                whose accent
could charm
            magpies
                    off the rocks
say, that discretion
is the better part of encounters
that have never been, noting a
likeness, a shadow, a throbbing
                hope nothing like the
        heft of very real
        purple potatoes
                in our haversack, say
        a kind word that
    crystallizes
            between our ears like
                        a branch
dropped
        into a salt
                mine
                begging
the question
                is the word real—is the branch
            real—is the mine
                        real?

        No, let the moment
        cool like a bit of
                    smelt
        because ordering a
        batch of Stendhal
        might not make a dent
        in memories of a prairie
        town outside of
                    Johannesburg

& the subjugated
reader must return
to the more reliable
heft of
purple
potatoes
in deft recitation
of our former
mantra:
the double helix hologram
on rear licence plate stalks
is the only real thing
in this freaking place

8

We return
to reality
take our time
around
Amisk
Lake
stop to
admire suckers
& jackfish
(together at last)
still wary of
bears
& what cannot be
suppressed
the vital
force of every letter, off-
kilter impulses
& impressions recently picked
in spite of frost warnings, luscious
images confined to nibbling, that
voluptuous
gush, that heap
of warm recriminations
upon subjective
chair
of marble eggs
where
the *Blessed Ludovica Albertoni*
clutches her least sinister breast
writhing in her ecstasy
over a bit of pre-volcanic tapestry
that tricks the eye that sees the neck-
ring of red cedar being fastened
around our seditious napes
in the name of civilization
leaving oscillations of
swelling affection that

teach the true value

                  of barter

yet chiefly that

      here

    among tundra swans
  with strange
     undulations
            ridge
        (the   on his bill
    a veritable
  gonflation of
     desire
    during breeding
          season)
here in the jewel
  of all this jagged
    boreality

     a pelican
  appears
      & Surrealism
         is born

MIGRATORY
LIBERTIES[*]

---

* Transmutation of "De la fleur d'amour et des chevaux migrateurs" by Robert Desnos.

In the forest an enormous flower dared
     to petrify every tree with love
Every tree loved this
Oaks toward midnight turned reptiles and crept along its stalk
Ashes and poplars curved toward its whorl
Ferns yellowed in the earth
Brighter than nocturnal love of sea and moon
Fainter than great volcanoes snuffed by this star
Sadder and more nostalgic than sand that dries
     dampens for finicky tide
I mean flower of the forest, not towers
I mean flower of the forest, not my love
Too faint and nostalgic and adorable
     loved by trees and ferns
     my breath left upon lips
     we are of the same essence
Encountered one day
I mean flower, not trees
In the tremulous forest where I walked
You, butterfly, died in its whorl
And you, fern, spoilt my heart
And you, my eyes, nearly fern, nearly coal, nearly flame
     nearly tide
In vain, I mean flower, I mean me
Ferns have yellowed on the ground to moonishness
Like the precise instant of lost agony between cornflower
     and a rose and yet a pearl
The sky is not so closed
A man crops up, announces his name – doors
     open, a chrysanthemum in his buttonhole
I mean immobile flower
     not ports of adventure and solitude
Trees, one by one, perish around the flower
Living upon their decay
That is why the plain fructified like membrane
Why cities cropped up

Stream at my feet curling up, waiting for my gratitude
　　　strand of greeting images
Somewhere a heart stops beating and the flower sticks up
Scent of flower succeeding time
Flower revealing its existence upon deflowered plain
　　　akin to moon or sea
　　　or arid atmosphere of spent hearts
A very red lobster claw rests beside the pot
The sun casts shadow of candle and flame
The flower sticks up with pride in fabled sky
Your nails, friends, are like its petals and pinks
The murmuring forest down there opens up
Heart akin to dehydrated spring
No more time, no more time to love
　　　you who take this road
The flower of the forest I recount is a chrysanthemum
The trees are dead the fields are green the cities are here
The great migratory bison horn the edges of distant fences
Soon the great bison thunder off
Cities watch them stampede in the street
　　　where stone echoes the heft of their hooves
　　　sometimes sparks
The fields are overturned by this cavalcade
Tufts of their tails loiter in the dust
　　　nostrils fuming in front of the flower·
For ages their shadows persist
But what happened to the migratory bison
　　　whose mottled coat was a cry for help
Sometimes you find a strange fossil buried in the earth
　　　one of their chalky bones
The flower that sees them still flourishes, stainless and strong
Leaves appear along its stalk
Ferns blaze and incline toward windows
But what became of the trees
Why did the flower flourish
Volcanoes! O Volcanoes!
The sky collapses
I dwell upon the distant, even deeper than me
Abolished times are like nails torn in slammed doors

When in the country a churl is near death, surrounded
by ripe fruit of late autumn by noisy frost
cracking upon faded panes with boredom
like cornflowers upon grass
The migratory bison crop up
When a traveller wanders among withered sprites
with wrinkled brows who retire in moving terrain
The migratory bison crop up
When a girl sleeps naked at the foot of a birch and waits
The migratory bison crop up
Appear in a rumble of broken flasks and creaking closets
Disappear in a hollow
No border has kept their back or gleaming rump
from reflecting sky
They pass, splashing freshly refashioned walls
And frost cracks ripe fruit plucked flowers rotting
sluggish terrain of bog slowly moulding
Watching the stride of migratory bison
Migratory bison
Migratory bison
Migratory bison
Migratory bison

ACKNOWLEDGEMENTS

Thank you to everyone at Talonbooks, especially Leslie Thomas Smith for his thoughtfulness on the design and to Charles Simard, whose intriguing queries resulted in several new transmutations.

Thank you to Clarise Foster for her continual friendship and her conscientious eyes on this text.

Thank you to Carleigh Baker, Michael Boughn, Weyman Chan, George Elliott Clarke, Méira Cook, Jamella Hagen, Jan Horner, Catherine Hunter, Emily Izsak, Sharon Thesen, and Jan Zwicky, all of whom have offered encouraging words for fragments of the urtext over the years. Thank you to Di Brandt for directing me to Charles Mair and his poem, "The Last Bison," and thank you Gregory Gibson for always providing impeccable editorial advice.

Thank you to *Cordite Poetry Review*, *Cough*, *Dispatches*, *Prairie Fire*, and *Surrealist Star Clustered Illuminations* for publishing early versions of the poems from this book.

Thank you to Stasja Voluti for her camaraderie and for her lovely images soaked in (a)ether.

GARRY THOMAS MORSE's six books of poetry include a homage to San Francisco Renaissance poet Jack Spicer in *After Jack* and an intensive exploration of his ancestral First Nations history in *Discovery Passages*, finalist for the Governor General's Award for Poetry and the Dorothy Livesay Poetry Prize. *Discovery Passages* was also voted One of the Top Ten Poetry Collections of 2011 by *The Globe and Mail* and One of the Best Ten Aboriginal Books from the past decade by CBC's *8th Fire*.

Morse's four books of fiction include the collection *Death in Vancouver*, and the three books in The Chaos! Quincunx series: 2013 ReLit Award finalist *Minor Episodes / Major Ruckus*, 2014 ReLit Award finalist *Rogue Cells / Carbon Harbour*, and *Minor Expectations*.

Since relocating from the West Coast to the Canadian prairie, Morse has written two books of poetry about this diverse landscape. These include Governor General's Award finalist *Prairie Harbour*, a long poem based on his year of living in Saskatchewan, and this volume, *Safety Sand*, a celebration of prairie surrealism.

Morse currently resides in Winnipeg, Manitoba, and is honoured to serve as the 2017–2018 Jack McClelland Writer-in-Residence at the University of Toronto.